EP Ancient History Printables: Levels 5-8

This book belongs to:

____

This book was made for your convenience. It is available for printing from the Easy Peasy All-in-One Homeschool website. It contains all of the printables from Easy Peasy's ancient history course for levels 5-8. The instructions for each page are found in the online course.

Easy Peasy All-in-One Homeschool is a free online homeschool curriculum providing high quality education for children around the globe. It provides complete courses for preschool through high school graduation. For EP's curriculum visit allinonehomeschool.com.

EP Ancient History Printables: Levels 5-8

This workbook, made by Elizabeth Mogg with permission from Easy Peasy All-in-One Homeschool, is based on the ancient history levels 5-8 component of Easy Peasy's curriculum. For EP's online curriculum visit allinonehomeschool.com.

ISBN: 9781080441198

First Edition: July 2019

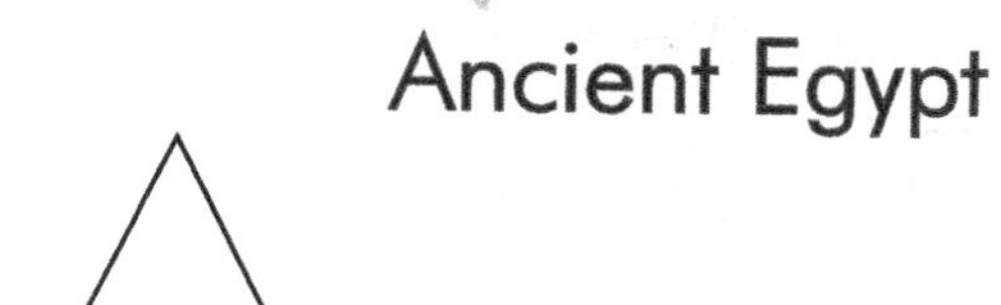

Ancient Egypt

The Old Kingdom

The Middle Kingdom

The New Kingdom

Timeline

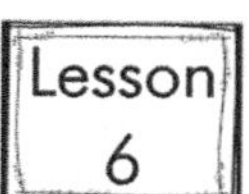

Rosetta Stone

Sphinx

Embalming the Pharaoh

Fill in the blanks to complete the sentences.

A paper made from a grassy reed is called

◻	♋	◻	⍓	❒	◆	⬧

In Ancient Egypt, the Pharaoh was believed to be a

♑	□	♎

When the Pharaoh died, the body was prepared for burial. The embalming process required certain organs to be removed and placed into jars. Using clues from your answers above and your knowledge of organs in the body, decipher the label on the jars to determine which organ each jar contains.

Some organs were NOT placed into jars. Cross out the names of the organs found on the labels to see which organs were not placed into jars.

BRAIN	STOMACH	LIVER
INTESTINES	HEART	LUNGS

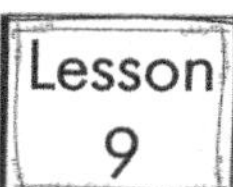

Notebooking Page

Egypt

Label the map.

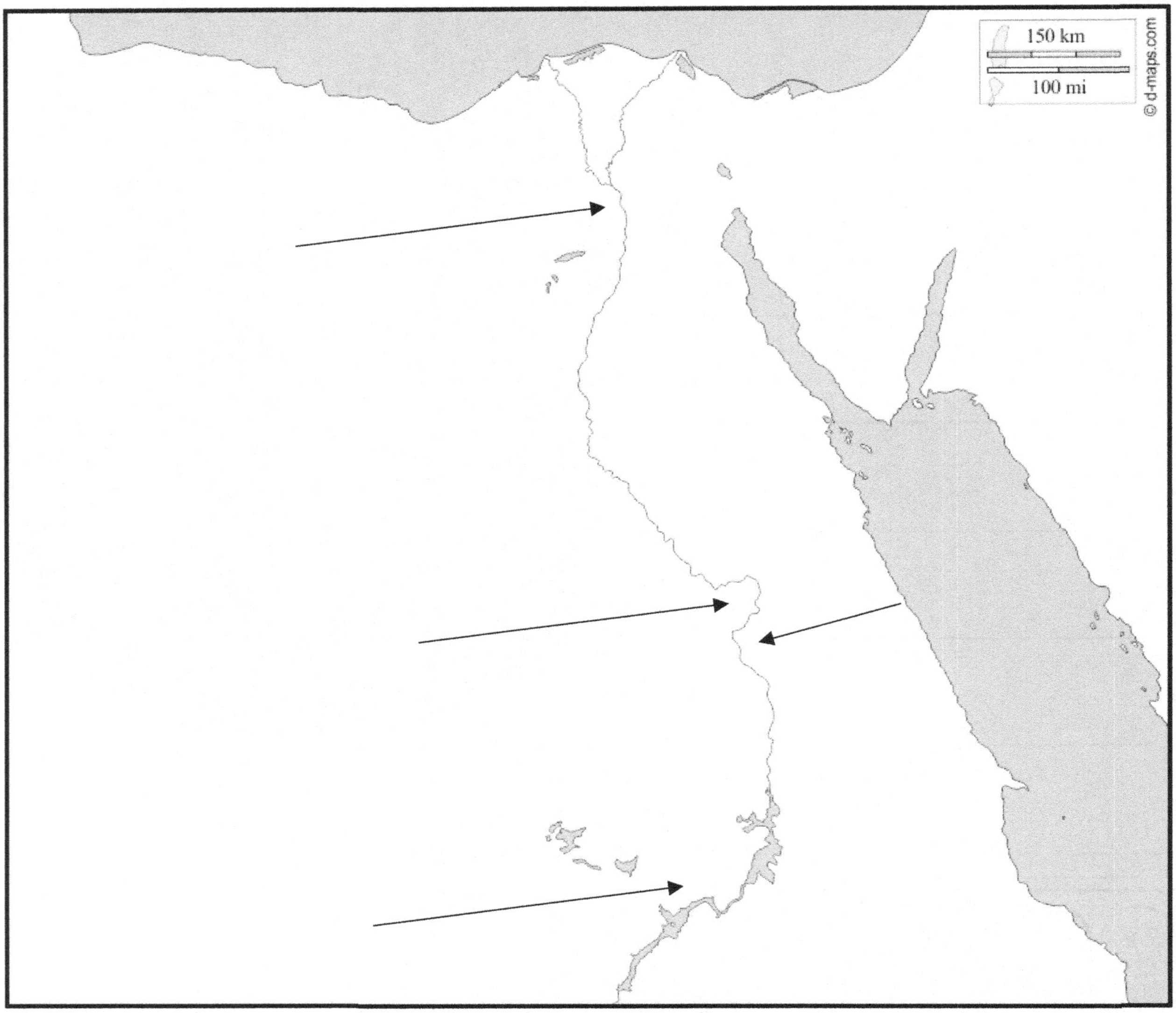

150 km
100 mi
© d-maps.com

Map Source: https://d-maps.com/m/africa/nil/nil03.gif

Ancient Egypt Timeline

Date	Political, Social Or Economic Change	Science or Religion	Literature	Architecture, Music, Art

Hidden Treasure

Answer the following questions to discover the hidden treasure. Once you have all the answers, follow the instructions at the bottom of the page to see if you found the treasure! (If you need help, there's a word bank at the bottom of the page.)

Mesopotamia means "between the ______________"

★					

Nebuchadnezzar had the Hanging Gardens of Babylon built for Queen ___________________.

★						

There were how many "Wonders of the Ancient World"?

★				

What was the name for a Mesopotamian temple tower?

★							

What kind of writing did the Sumerians invent?

★								

The area once known as Babylon is in modern day _____________.

★			

Now that you have all your answers, write the letters in the starred boxes in order on the blank below (no spaces or punctuation, just the letters from each box):

allinonehomeschool.com/_________________

Enter this address in your browser (use all lowercase letters) to see if you got all the questions correct and found the treasure. (If you get a message that says "oops, that page can't be found" you should go back and check your answers!)

WORD BANK		
Iraq	Amyitis	rivers
Ziggurat	seven	cuneiform

Compare and Contrast Hammurabi's Laws

Choose 3 of Hammurabi's laws. Explain the law in your own words. Compare and contrast each law with a law or laws we have today.

Law 1:	
Similar to a current law:	Different from a current law:
Law 2:	
Similar to a current law:	Different from a current law:
Law 3:	
Similar to a current law:	Different from a current law:

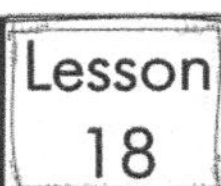

Mesopotamia Timeline

Date	Political, Social Or Economic Change	Science or Religion	Literature	Architecture, Music, Art

Current Events

Answer each question about the article you read.

What happened?

Who was there?

When did it happen?

Where did it happen?

Why did it happen?

China Timeline

Date	Political, Social Or Economic Change	Science or Religion	Literature	Architecture, Music, Art

China Timeline

Date	Political, Social Or Economic Change	Science or Religion	Literature	Architecture, Music, Art

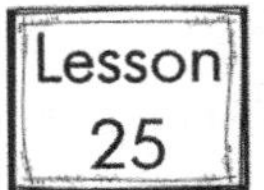

The Great Wall of China

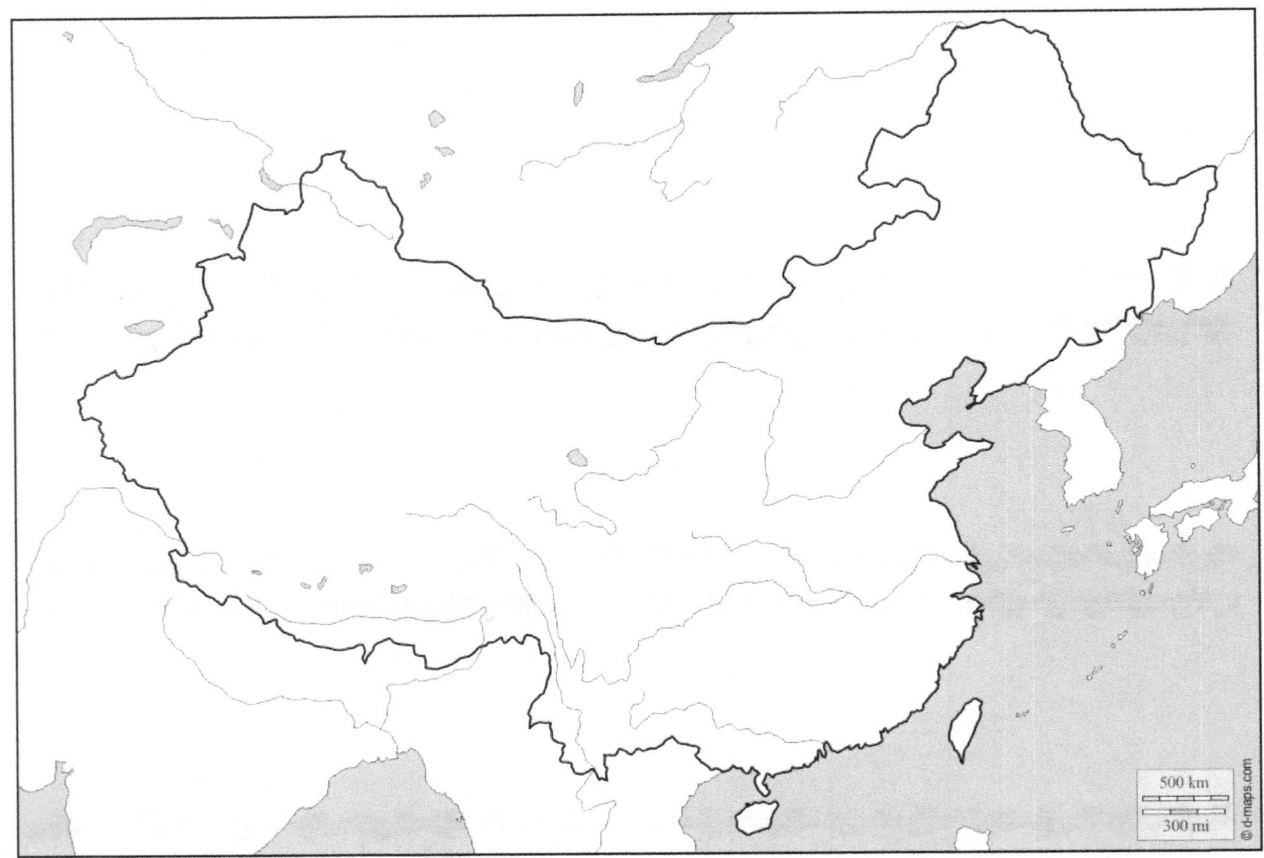

Source: https://d-maps.com/m/asia/china/chine/chine13.gif

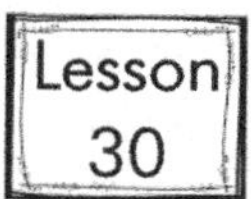

Silk Road

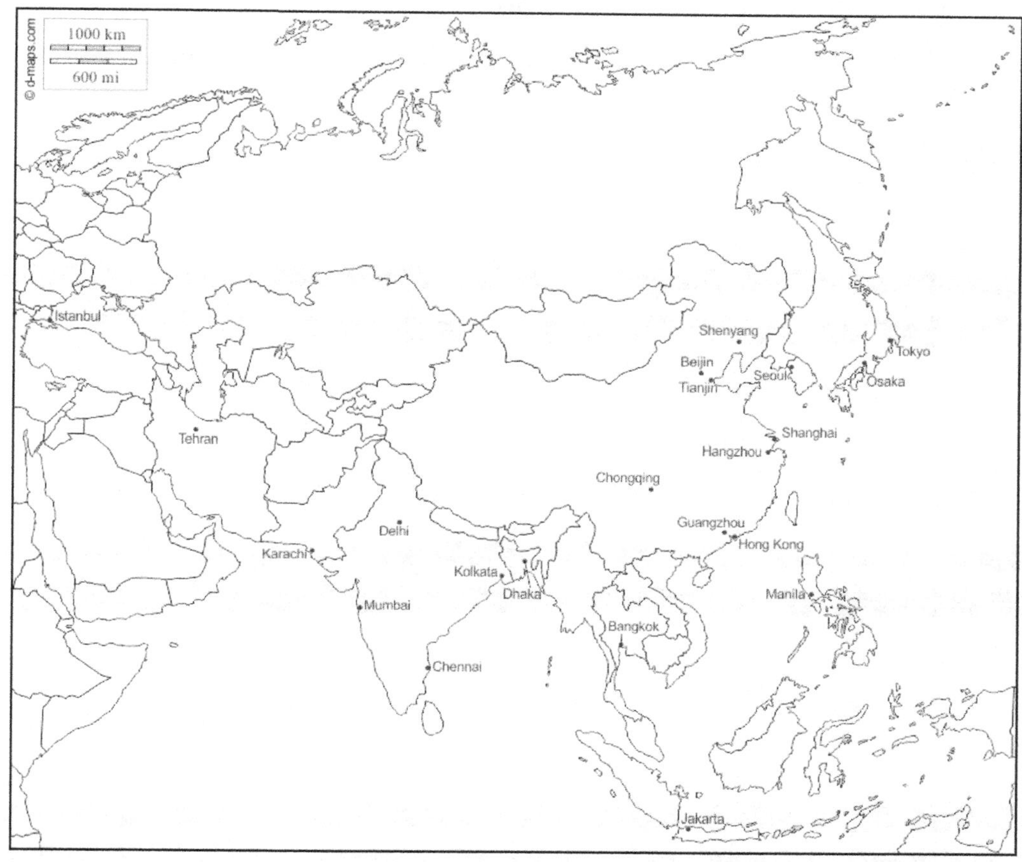

Source: https://d-maps.com/m/asia/asie/asie32.gif

Indus Valley Timeline

Date	Political, Social Or Economic Change	Science or Religion	Literature	Architecture, Music, Art

Current Events

What happened?

Who was there?

When did it happen?

Where did it happen?

Why did it happen?

Ancient Greece

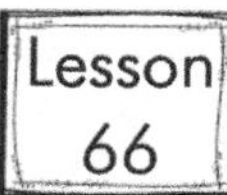

Hidden Treasure

Answer the following questions to discover the hidden treasure. Once you have all the answers, follow the instructions at the bottom of the page to see if you found the treasure! (If you need help, there's a word bank at the bottom of the page.)

Who fought Athens in the Peloponnesian War?

★					

The Olympics were held every ______________ years.

★			

An Olympic event consisting of discus, javelin, jumping, running and wrestling:

★									

An Olympic event that was basically free-for-all fighting:

★									

Greeks believed 12 main gods lived on Mount ____________________.

★						

A Greek philosopher famous for his "dialogues."

★				

Now that you have all your answers, write the letters in the starred boxes in order on the blank below (no spaces or punctuation, just the letters from each box):

allinonehomeschool.com/______________

Enter this address in your browser (use all lowercase letters) to see if you got all the questions correct and found the treasure. (If you get a message that says "oops, that page can't be found" you should go back and check your answers!)

WORD BANK		
Plato	Sparta	pankration
pentathlon	four	Olympus

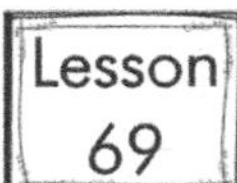

Greece Timeline

Date	Political, Social Or Economic Change	Science or Religion	Literature	Architecture, Music, Art

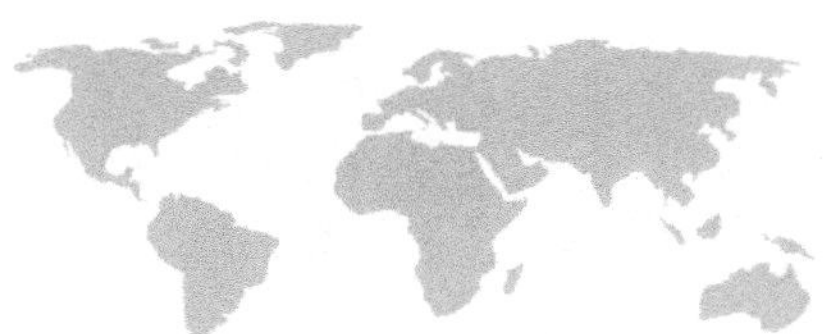

Current Events

Who was there?

What happened?

When did it happen?

Where did it happen?

Why did it happen?

Hidden Treasure

Answer the following questions to discover the hidden treasure. Once you have all the answers, follow the instructions at the bottom of the page to see if you found the treasure! (If you need help, there's a word bank at the bottom of the page.)

At the time of the Romans, France was known by what name?

★			

What were volunteer gladiators called?

★								

Structures that brought fresh water in and carried waste water away:

★								

Who ran Roman government and society?

★		

What is the Latin word for circle?

★					

Now that you have all your answers, write the letters in the starred boxes in order on the blank below (no spaces or punctuation, just the letters from each box):

allinonehomeschool.com/______________

Enter this address in your browser (use all lowercase letters) to see if you got all the questions correct and found the treasure. (If you get a message that says "oops, that page can't be found" you should go back and check your answers!)

WORD BANK		
circus	Auctorati	men
aqueducts		Gaul

Current Events

What happened?

When did it happen?

Where did it happen?

Who was there?

Why did it happen?

Map Activity

The region of Denmark, Norway, and Sweden is known by another name.

Unscramble these letters and write the name of the region: VDISANAICAN

____

Place an X on the area of the map that shows the Vikings' homeland.

Label the bodies of water to the east and west of the Vikings' homeland.

Choose a different color to represent each area listed in the Map Key. Color that area on the map with the correct color.

Map Key	
	Denmark
	Norway
	Sweden

500 km
300 mi
© d-maps.com

Map source: https://d-maps.com/m/europa/europemax/europemax09.gif

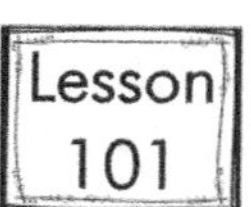

Hidden Treasure

Answer the following questions to discover the hidden treasure. Once you have all the answers, follow the instructions at the bottom of the page to see if you found the treasure! (If you need help, there's a word bank at the bottom of the page.)

Leif Ericson landed in North America somewhere in the area we call Canada.
What did he call the area?

★						

What were the scariest Vikings called?

★									

What is the Viking weapon of choice?
(Used for throwing and fighting)

★		

What is named after the Viking god Odin?

★								

What is the name of the runic alphabet used to write the Old Norse (Viking) language?

★						

Now that you have all your answers, write the letters in the starred boxes in order on the blank below (no spaces or punctuation, just the letters from each box):

allinonehomeschool.com/______________

Enter this address in your browser (use all lowercase letters) to see if you got all the questions correct and found the treasure. (If you get a message that says "oops, that page can't be found" you should go back and check your answers!)

WORD BANK		
axe	Wednesday	Berserkers
Vinland		Futhark

Directions: Winner is the first to reach all twelve destinations. Roll one die or draw numbered pieces of paper. Move that many spaces. A space is any connected country or body of water. Check off each destination when you reach it.

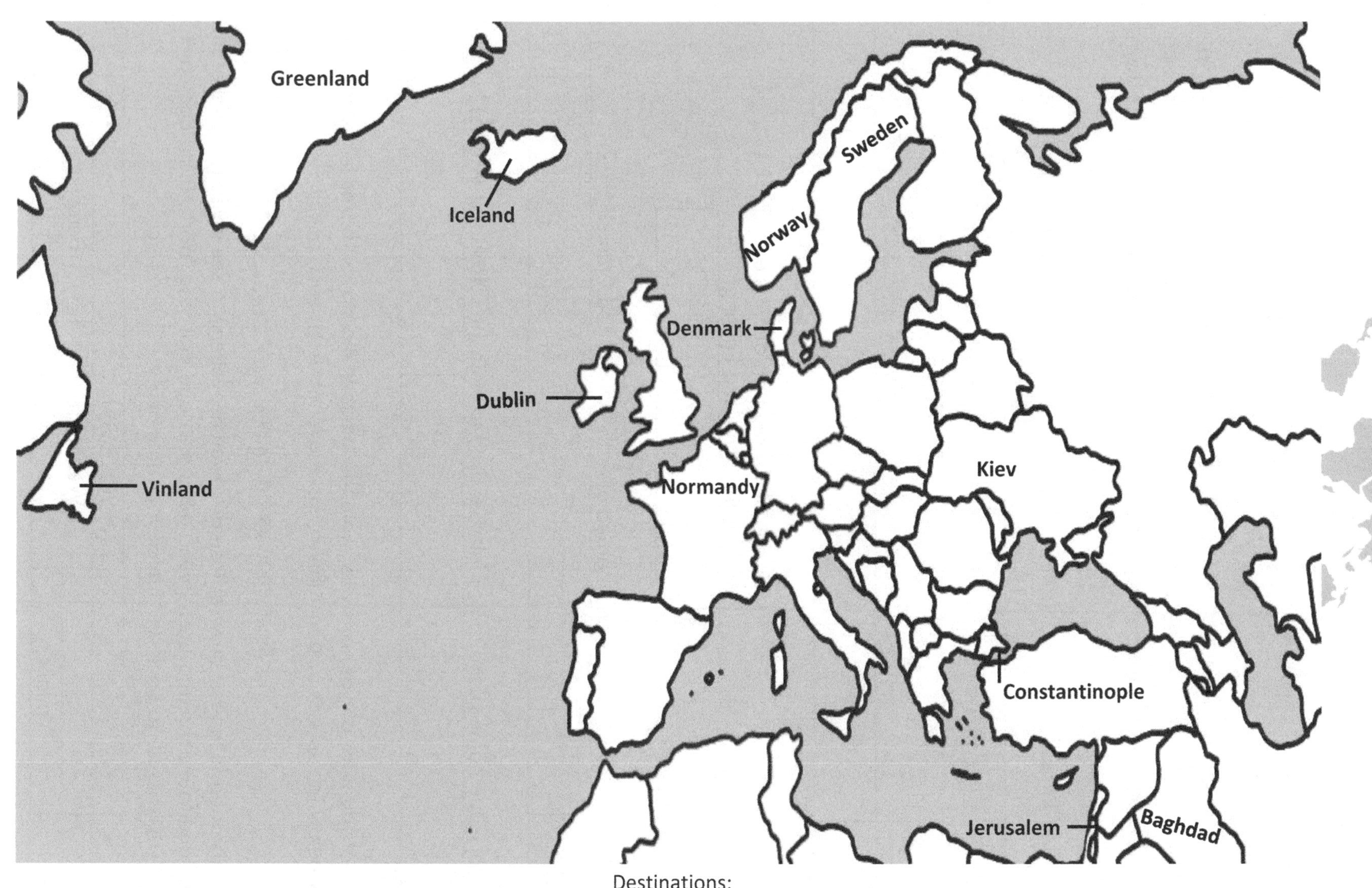

Destinations:

Vinland – Greenland – Iceland – Dublin – Normandy – Denmark – Norway – Sweden – Kiev – Constantinople – Jerusalem - Baghdad

Vikings Timeline

Date	Political, Social Or Economic Change	Science or Religion	Literature	Architecture, Music, Art

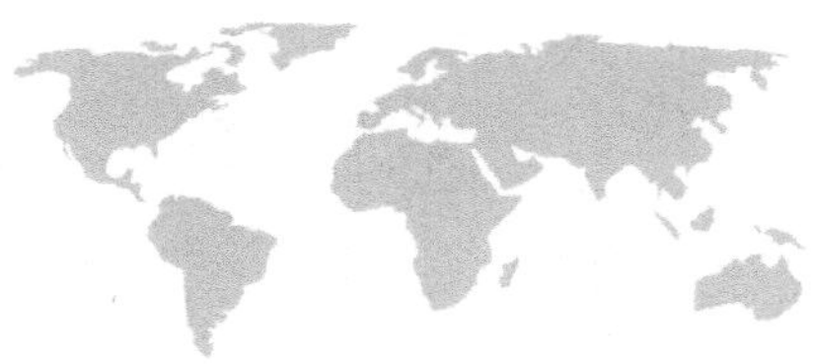

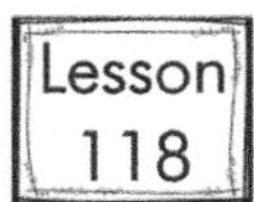

Crusades

Fill in the table to help you write a newspaper article about the Crusades.

Headline: (A short statement to grab the reader's attention)	
Byline: (The name of the author of the article: YOU!)	
Lead paragraph: (Write a sentence to answer each of these questions.)	
Who?	
What?	
When?	
Where?	
Why?	
How?	
Explanation: Other facts or details the reader would want to know	
Additional information: Extra information that does not need to be included but can be added if the article needs to be longer.	

Venn Diagram

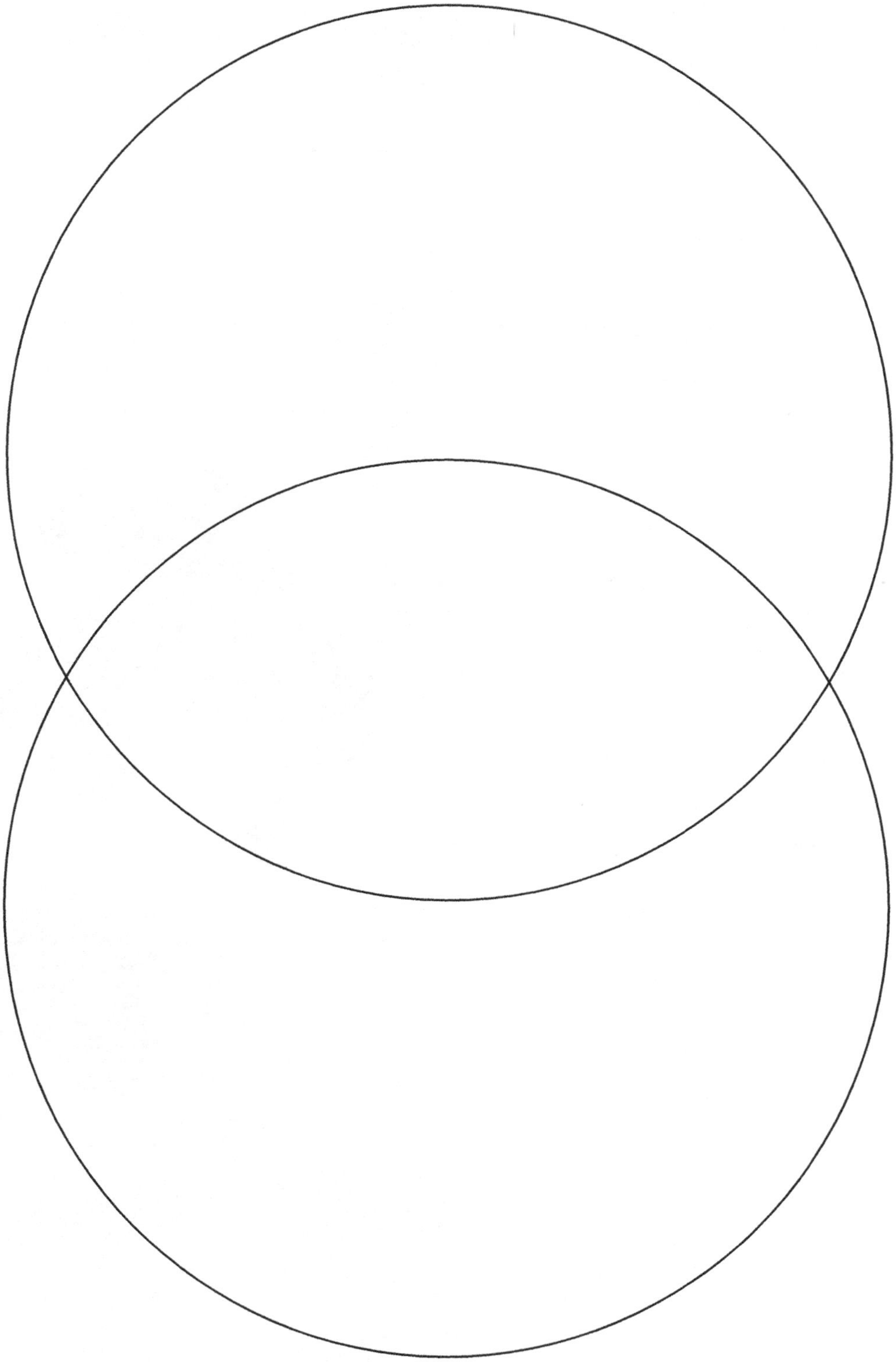

Notebooking Page

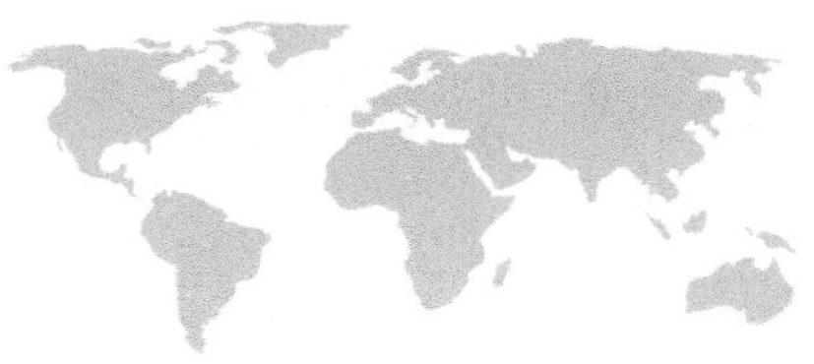

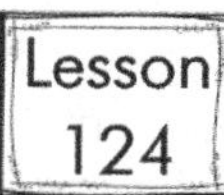

Hidden Treasure

Answer the following questions to discover the hidden treasure. Once you have all the answers, follow the instructions at the bottom of the page to see if you found the treasure! (If you need help, there's a word bank at the bottom of the page.)

In the 17th Century, Tokugawa Ieyusa rules Japan.
He was called ________________.

★					

What is the name of Japanese poetry consisting of 17 syllables set up in groups of 5, 7, 5?

★				

What is the name of the Samurai Code of Honor?

★						

What is the name of the belt on a kimono?

★		

What is a dish made from the poisonous puffer fish?

★			

Now that you have all your answers, write the letters in the starred boxes in order on the blank below (no spaces or punctuation, just the letters from each box):

allinonehomeschool.com/______________

Enter this address in your browser (use all lowercase letters) to see if you got all the questions correct and found the treasure. (If you get a message that says "oops, that page can't be found" you should go back and check your answers!)

WORD BANK		
Bushido	Shogun	obi
fugu		haiku

Current Events

Who?

What?

Where?

When?

Why?

Genghis Khan

Genghis Khan Timeline

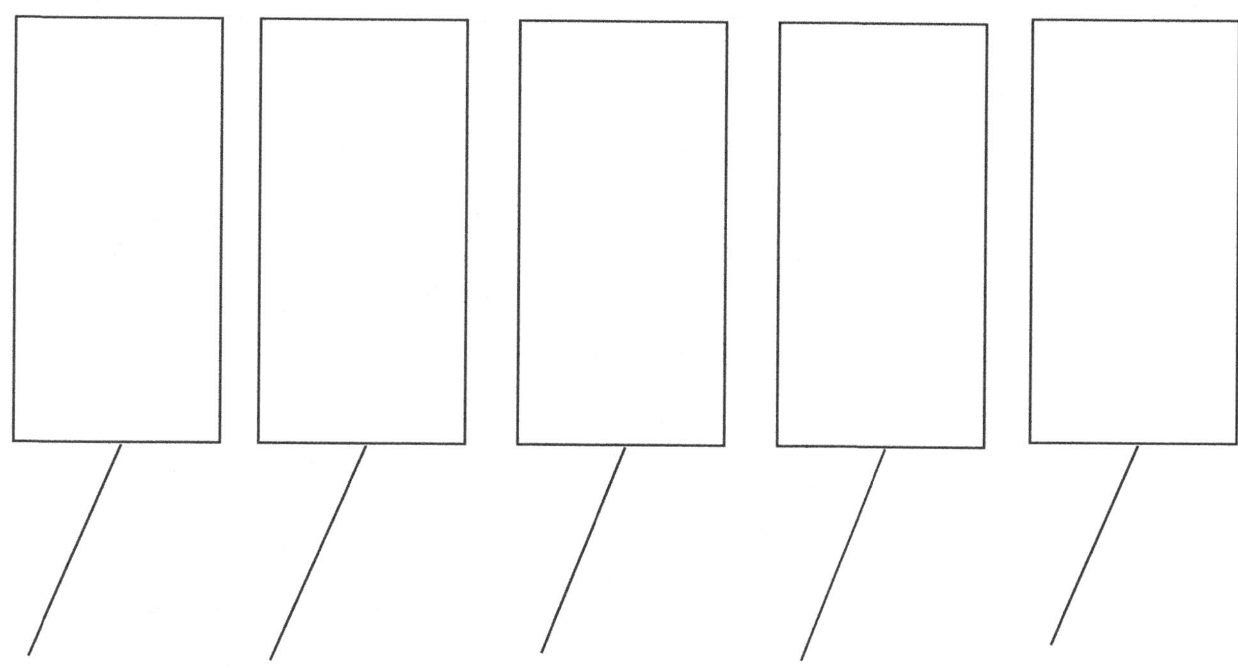

Hidden Treasure

Answer the following questions to discover the hidden treasure. Once you have all the answers, follow the instructions at the bottom of the page to see if you found the treasure! (If you need help, there's a word bank at the bottom of the page.)

Most people know him as Genghis Khan.
He was also called ________________.

★						

What was the most common mode of transportation?

★				

What is the name of the Mongolian game played using deer bones?

★					

What is a popular sport in Mongolia?

★								

As nomadic people, Mongolians used tents known as gers or ____________.

★				

Now that you have all your answers, write the letters in the starred boxes in order on the blank below (no spaces or punctuation, just the letters from each box):

allinonehomeschool.com/______________

Enter this address in your browser (use all lowercase letters) to see if you got all the questions correct and found the treasure. (If you get a message that says "oops, that page can't be found" you should go back and check your answers!)

WORD BANK		
horse	Temujin	Shagai
wrestling		yurts

Current Events

Who?

What?

Where?

When?

Why?

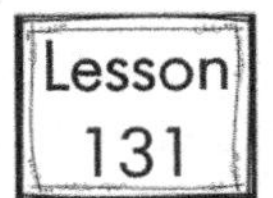

Ottoman Empire

Color the area showing where the Ottoman Empire ruled. Label Africa, Asia, and Europe.

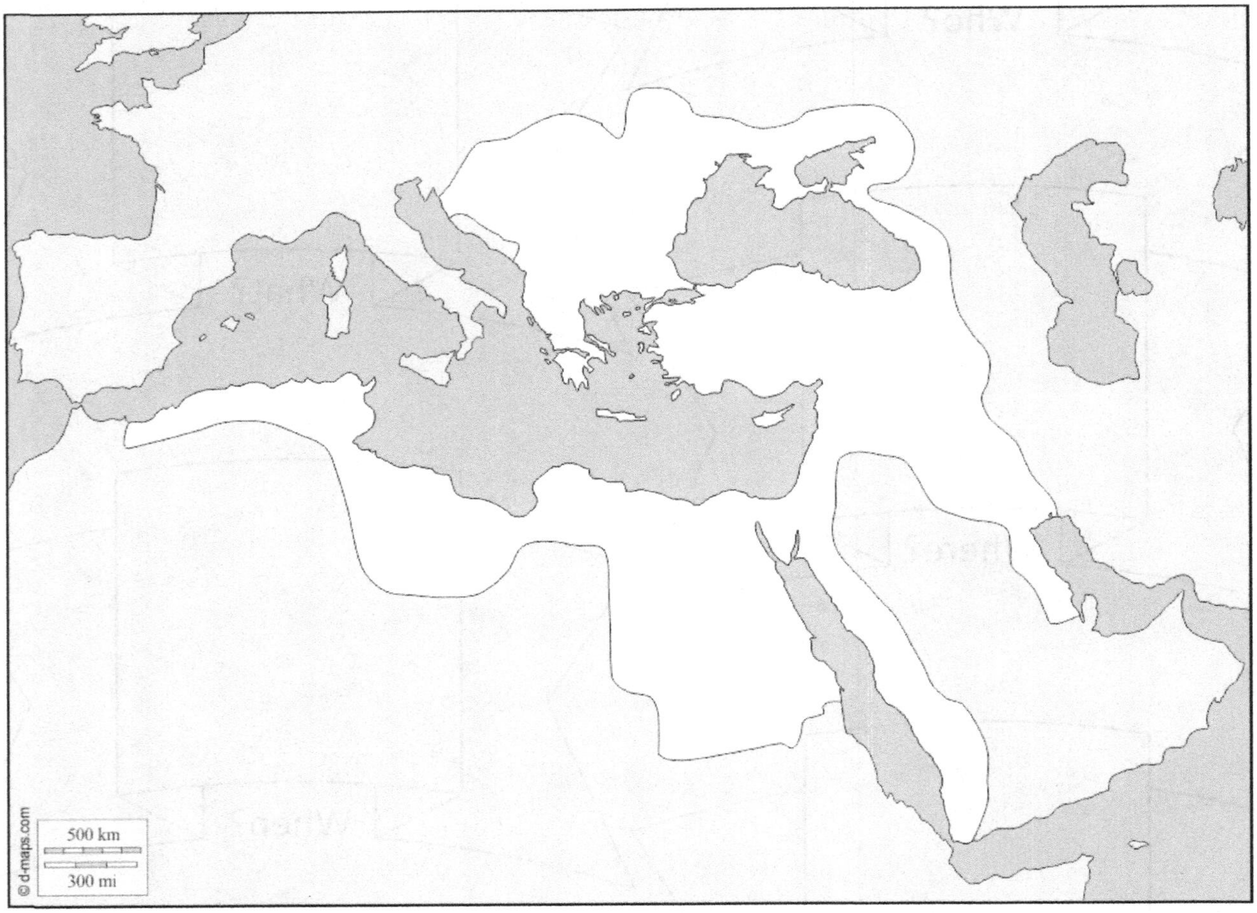

© d-maps.com
500 km
300 mi

https://d-maps.com/m/history/ottomans/ottomans03.gif

Hidden Treasures

Answer the following questions to discover the hidden treasure. Once you have all the answers, follow the instructions at the bottom of the page to see if you found the treasure! (If you need help, there's a word bank at the bottom of the page.)

In the 16th Century, Turkey was part of the ____________ Empire.

★						

The Sultan during the Ottoman Empire's most successful time period was ____________.

★							

The name of the government center of the Ottoman Empire was ____________ Palace.

★						

What is the name of a Muslim place of worship?

★					

What provided the heat for the hot baths in the Haseki Hurrem baths?

★				

Now that you have all your answers, write the letters in the starred boxes in order on the blank below (no spaces or punctuation, just the letters from each box):

allinonehomeschool.com/____________

Enter this address in your browser (use all lowercase letters) to see if you got all the questions correct and found the treasure. (If you get a message that says "oops, that page can't be found" you should go back and check your answers!)

WORD BANK		
mosque	Ottoman	steam
Suleyman		Topkapi

Aztec Empire

Draw a picture of what you think Tenochtitlan looked like.

Describe life in the city of Tenochtitlan.

What did you learn about conquistadors?

Which conquistador arrived in the Aztec territory?

Describe what happened to the Aztec Empire.

Ancient History
Levels 5-8

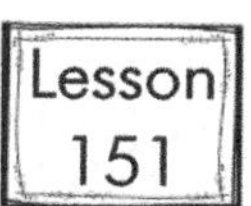

Hidden Treasures

Answer the following questions to discover the hidden treasure. Once you have all the answers, follow the instructions at the bottom of the page to see if you found the treasure! (If you need help, there's a word bank at the bottom of the page.)

A time of reborn interest in Roman and Greek styles of painting, sculpture, and architecture is known as the Italian ________________.

★										

Leonardo painted the "Mona Lisa" and "The Last ______________."

★					

Leonardo was known for writing ________________.

★								

Leonardo invented a cannon powered by ________

★				

Leonardo also worked as a military inventor for Cesare ________

★					

Now that you have all your answers, write the letters in the starred boxes in order on the blank below (no spaces or punctuation, just the letters from each box):

allinonehomeschool.com/____________

Enter this address in your browser (use all lowercase letters) to see if you got all the questions correct and found the treasure. (If you get a message that says "oops, that page can't be found" you should go back and check your answers!)

WORD BANK		
Supper	backwards	steam
Renaissance		Borgia

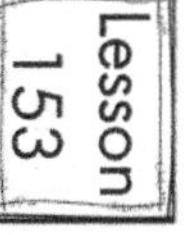

Choose a color to use to draw the route for each explorer.

- [ ] Magellan
- [ ] Drake
- [ ] Marco Polo
- [ ] Verrazano
- [ ] De Champlain
- [ ] Cabot
- [ ] Vasco Da Gama
- [ ] Ponce de Leon
- [ ] De Soto
- [ ] Hudson

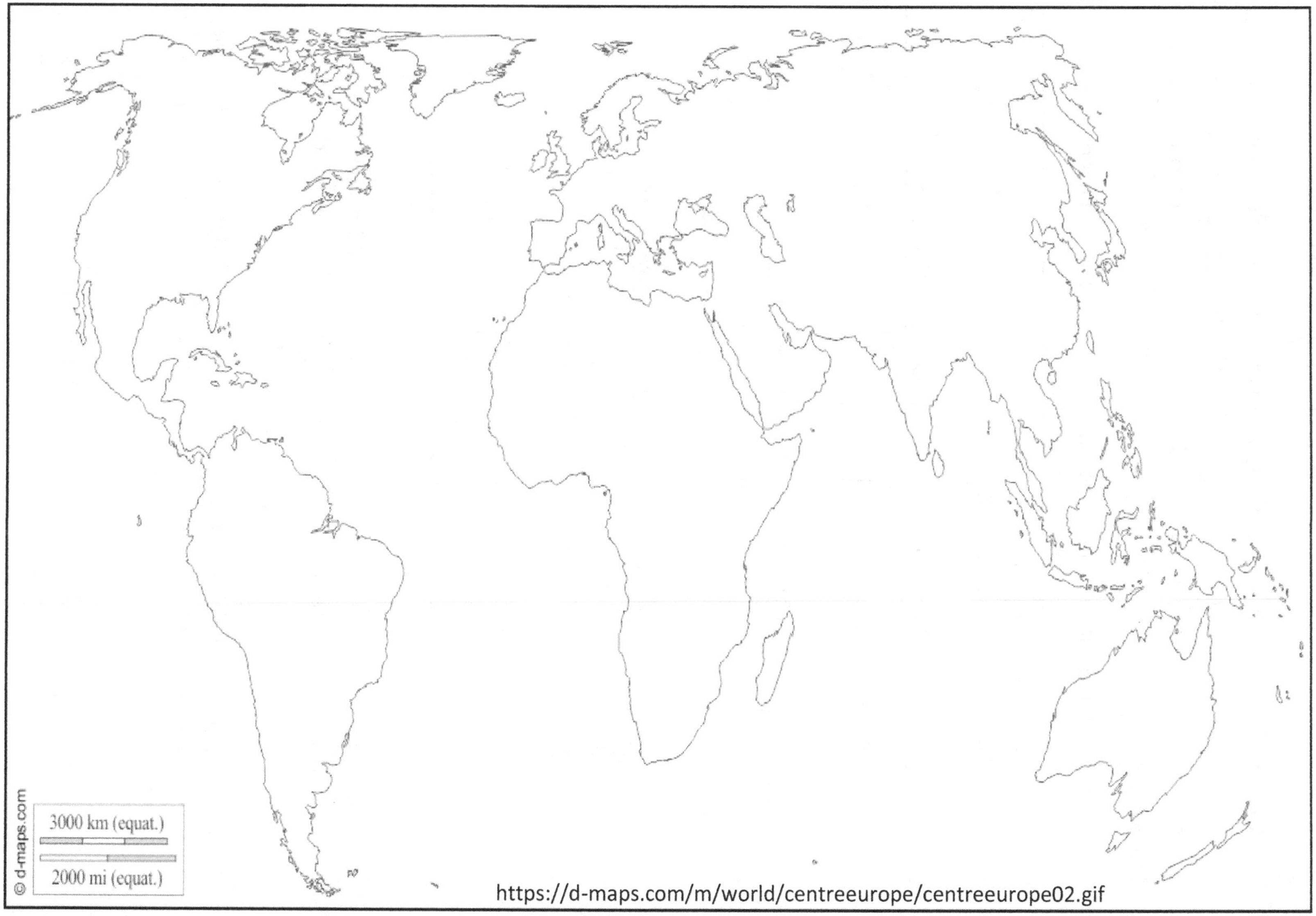

3000 km (equat.)

2000 mi (equat.)

https://d-maps.com/m/world/centreeurope/centreeurope02.gif

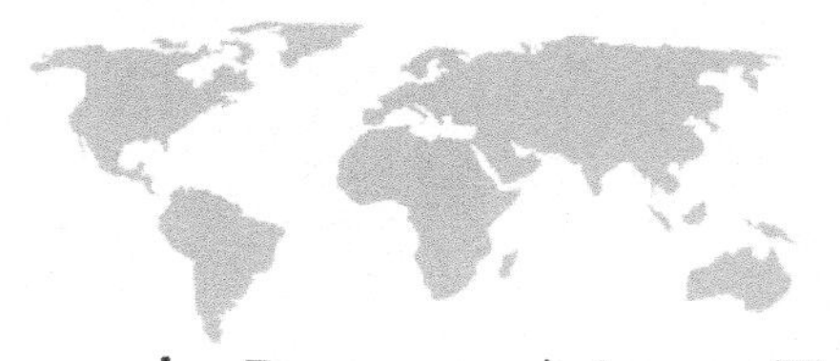

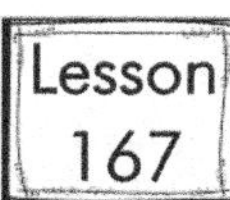

Research Report Note Taker

Topic: ______________________________

Resource 1: ______________________________

Info: ______________ Info: ______________

Info: ______________ Info: ______________

Info: ______________ Info: ______________

Resource 2: ______________________________

Info: ______________ Info: ______________

Info: ______________ Info: ______________

Info: ______________ Info: ______________

Resource 3: ______________________________

Info: ______________ Info: ______________

Info: ______________ Info: ______________

Info: ______________ Info: ______________

Resource 4: ______________________________

Info: ______________ Info: ______________

Info: ______________ Info: ______________

Info: ______________ Info: ______________

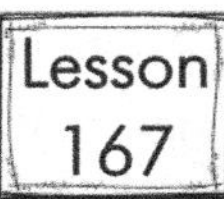

Resource 5: ______________________

Info: ____________ Info: ____________

Info: ____________ Info: ____________

Info: ____________ Info: ____________

Resource 6: ______________________

Info: ____________ Info: ____________

Info: ____________ Info: ____________

Info: ____________ Info: ____________

Resource 7: ______________________

Info: ____________ Info: ____________

Info: ____________ Info: ____________

Info: ____________ Info: ____________

Resource 8: ______________________

Info: ____________ Info: ____________

Info: ____________ Info: ____________

Info: ____________ Info: ____________

Resource 9: ______________________

Info: ____________ Info: ____________

Info: ____________ Info: ____________

Info: ____________ Info: ____________

Ancient Music Worksheets

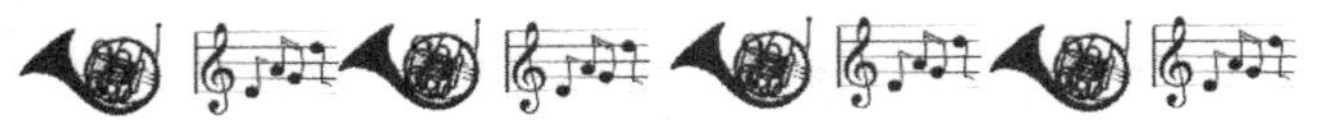

Ancient Roman Instruments

Mark which instruments you think you hear as you listen to the ancient Roman music of *Synaulia II*.

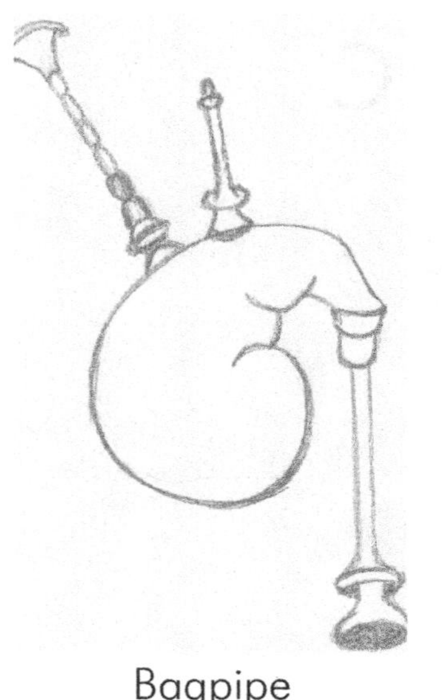

Bagpipe

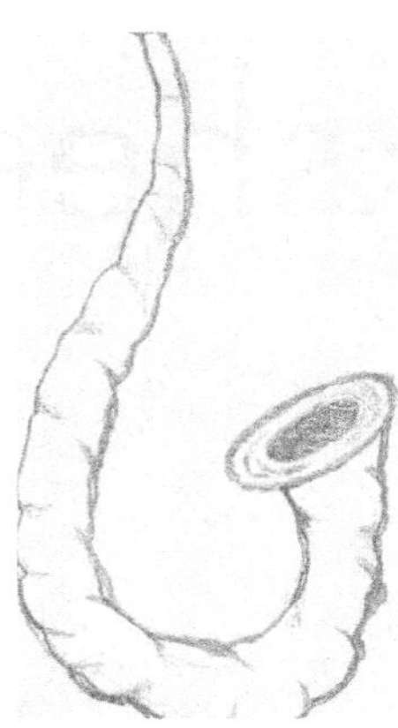

Buccina

Bugle

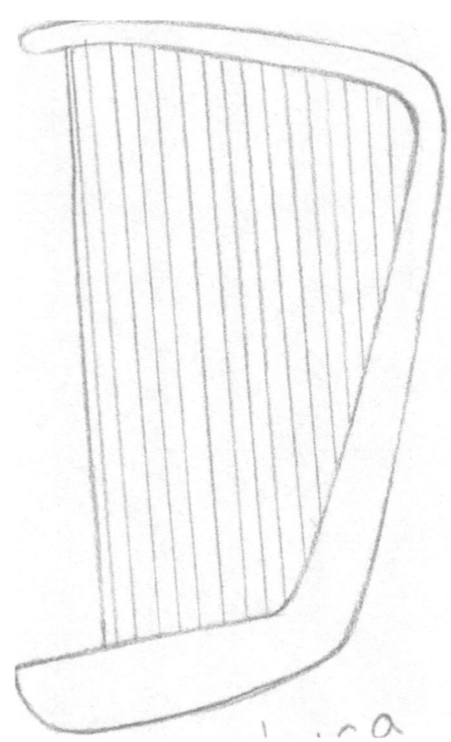

Sambuca

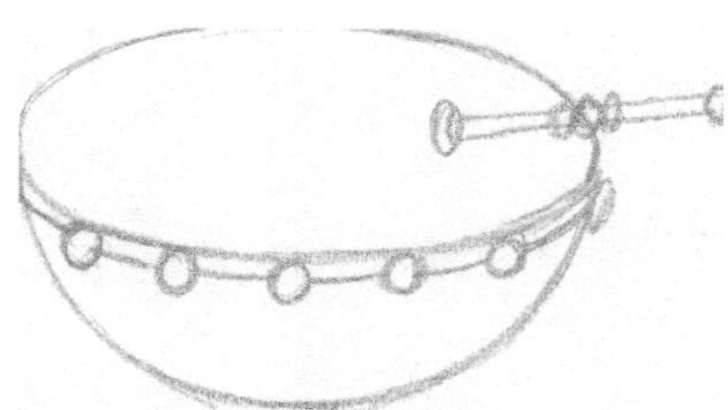

Tympanum

Aulos (wind instrument)

Medieval Instruments

Use this page to draw and write about your medieval instrument.

Instrument name: ______________________

____

____

____

____

____

Bible Worksheets

Ten Commandments

Write the commandment on the top if it is summed up by "love God" and on the bottom if it is summed up by "love your neighbor."

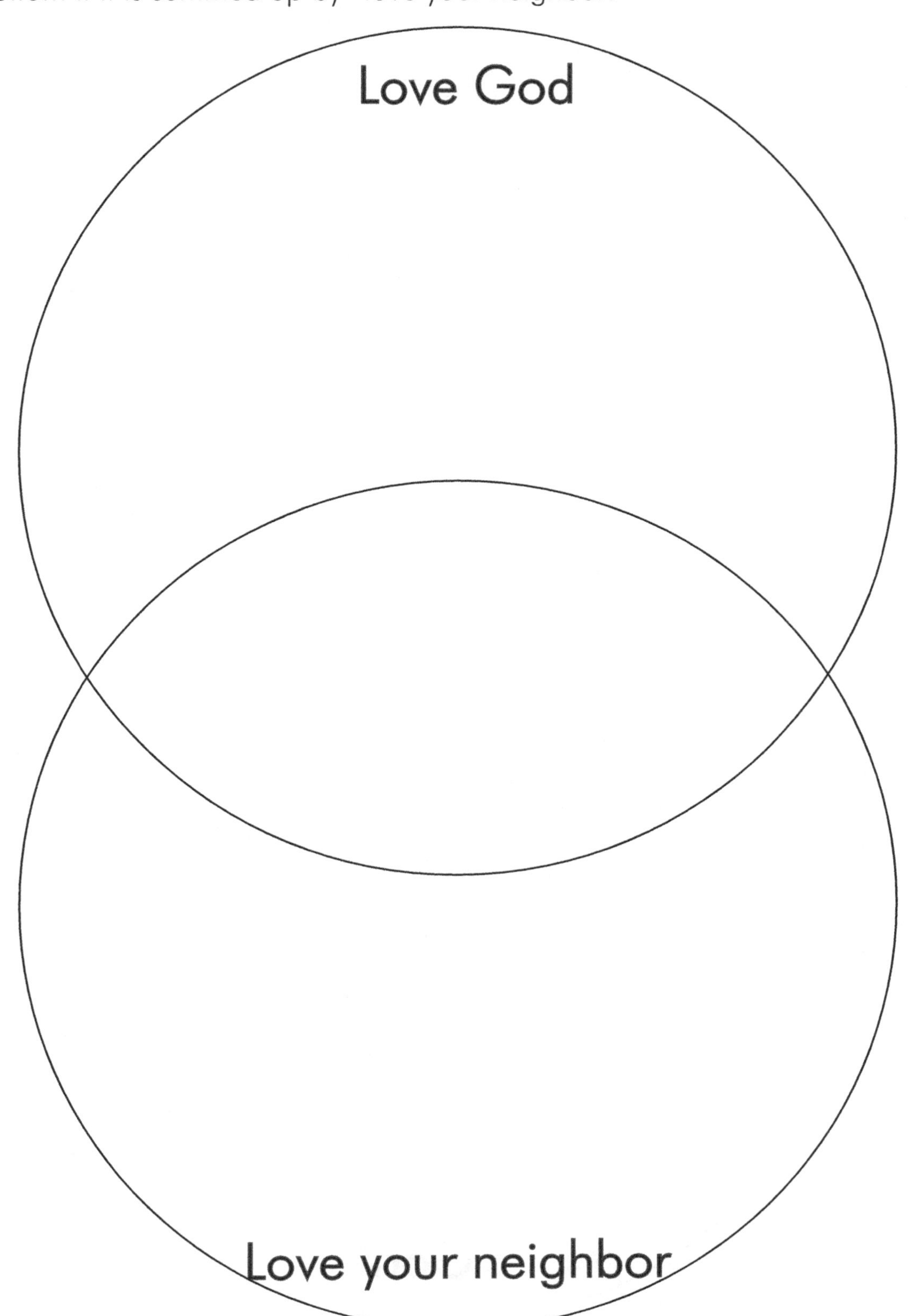

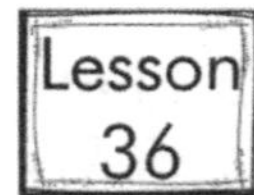

God and Man

On the top, write things about man. On the bottom, write things about God. In the middle, write what it shows about the relationship between God and man.

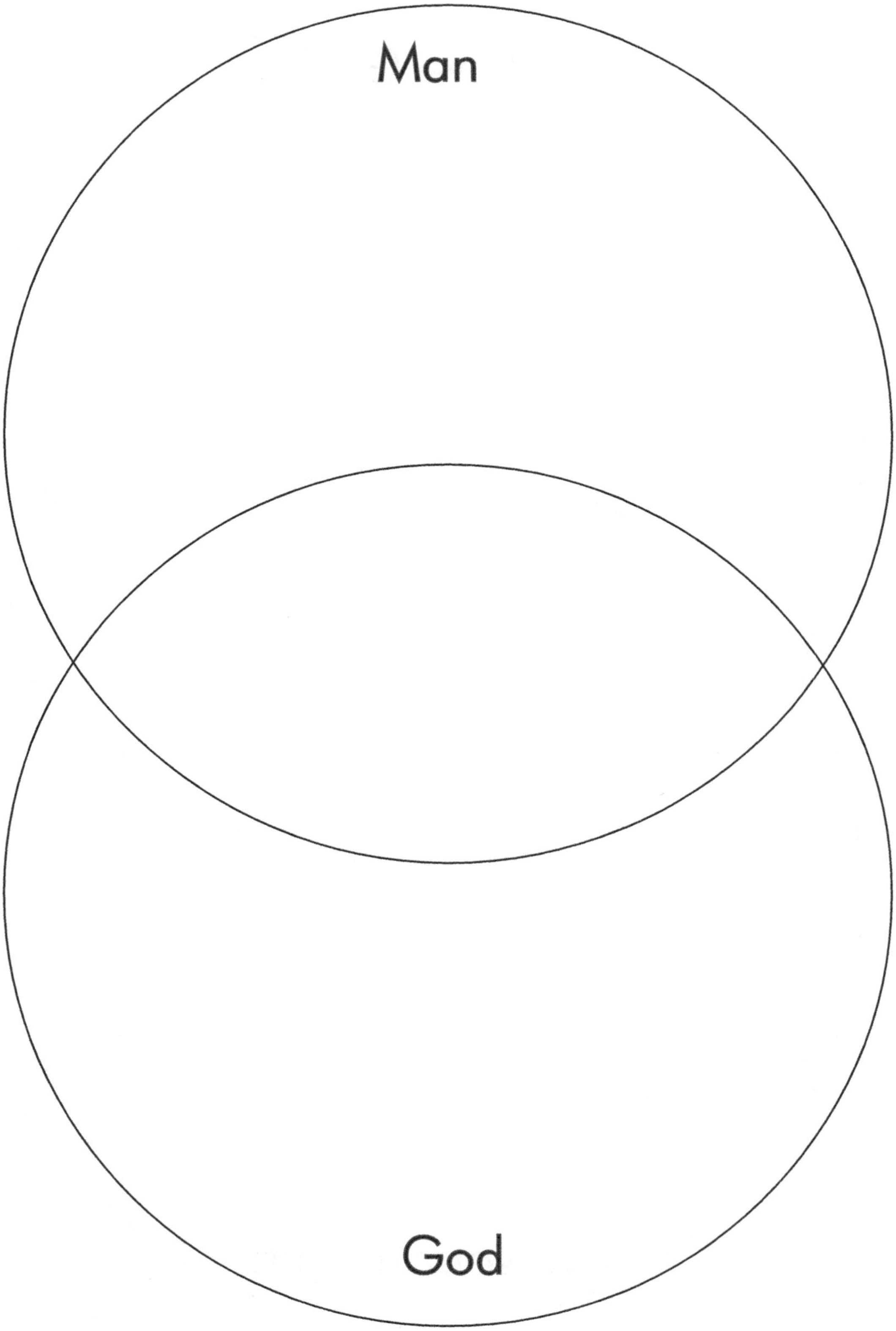

Man

God

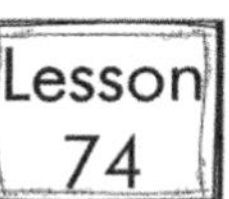

Ten Commandments

Fill in the Ten Commandments.

1. ______________________________
2. ______________________________
3. ______________________________
4. ______________________________
5. ______________________________
6. ______________________________
7. ______________________________
8. ______________________________
9. ______________________________
10. ______________________________

Made in United States
North Haven, CT
01 August 2023

39811749R00030